TAKING BACK YOUR
POWER
(21) SECRETS

TAKING BACK YOUR
POWER
(21) SECRETS

DR. TERRENCE PARRIS

XULON PRESS

Xulon Press
2301 Lucien Way #415
Maitland, FL 32751
407.339.4217
www.xulonpress.com

© 2018 by Dr. Terrence Parris

All rights reserved solely by the author. The author guarantees all contents are original and do not infringe upon the legal rights of any other person or work. No part of this book may be reproduced in any form without the permission of the author. The views expressed in this book are not necessarily those of the publisher.

Unless otherwise indicated, Scripture quotations taken from the King James Version (KJV) – *public domain*.

Printed in the United States of America.

ISBN-13: 978-1-5456-5106-3

AUTHOR'S NOTE

I, **Dr. Terrence Parris on Wednesday, September 19, 2012,** pledged to myself to TAKE BACK MY POWER. In order for me to accomplish this task, I began to write a set of goals which ended up being 21 Secrets expounding on the Word of God known as the His Holy Bible Scriptures, which bear witness to making these 21 Secrets come into full manifestation since God's Word is ALIVE and can never return VOID when activated by the Christian Believer.

ACKNOWLEDGEMENT

Firstly, I would like to thank my wonderful wife and daughter for their unselfish support and encouragement during the process of writing this book. My spiritual sons and daughters in the ministry for their prayers and encouragement. And all those who have supported me in this project through the process. To our Bible School students, past and present, thank you for allowing me to pour into your life the substance of God's Word. Thank you for believing in me. Lastly, a special thank you to all my Spiritual Mentors, and those that have transitioned, and those that are still alive and on the battle field for the Lord. You know who you are. Again, blessings to you all. To God be the glory for the great things He has done. Shalom!!!

CONTENTS

Author's Note v
Acknowledgement. vii
Preface xi
Introduction. xiii

Do Not Give Up, Because You Can Make It

Secret # 1 The Secret of Overcoming a Negative Mindset 2
Secret # 2 Where Do Your Negative Patterns Come From? 3
Secret # 3 Don't You Ever Go There! But Go to
The Place called "There" 4
Secret # 4 You Must Take the Power
Away from All Negativity. 5
Secret # 5 The Choice is Always Yours to Make 6
Secret # 6 Displace All Negative People Out of Your Life
and Replace Them with Positive People. 7

Failure Is Not A Choice

Secret # 7 Learn to Welcome Criticism 10
Secret # 8 Failure is Not to be Feared.
It is a Prerequisite to Your Success. .11
Secret # 9 Failure will Wake You Up
And Make You Strong. 12
Secret # 10 Failure Makes Winning Feel Better and
Taste Sweeter 13
Secret # 11 Failure Teaches Life Lessons. 14

Secret # 12 Dealing with Your Personal Failures
Effectively and Successfully............................ 15

Secret # 13 You Must Overcome
Your Negative Mindset................................ 16

Secret # 14 You Can Overcome Your Failures
by Developing the Right Mindset....................... 17

Make Your Work, Work for You

Secret # 15 You Don't Have to be a Slave to Work 20

Secret # 16 Your Work Does not have to be Work 21

Secret # 17 Just Go the Extra Mile, It Will Not Hurt 22

Secret # 18 When You Feel Overwhelmed,
Consider Doing Some Meditation 23

Secret # 19 Try Doing Positive Affirmations 24

Secret # 20 Fake It Until You Make It 25

Secret # 21 Making Positive Changes Is a Lifetime Habit.... 26

Conclusion 27

PREFACE

Power

The word of God lets us know that "God has not given us a spirit of fear; but of love, power and a sound mind." (2 Timothy 1:17) The Oxford English Dictionary defines power as the ability to direct or influence the behaviour of others or the course of events.

As human beings, we struggle with the concept of power, because we all desire to manipulate the behavior of others. We desire to influence the actions of others, whether it be in a positive or negative manner.

Our goal in life is to assert our authority over those we deem less privileged than ourselves. Some of us have a need to be in control of every situation. The need for dominance often causes an imbalance in our relationships.

We must be cautious when we utilize our capacity to have an impact on the lives of others because we can damage potential and growth. The word of God says, "We should esteem others higher than ourselves." (Philippians 2:3) In so doing, we tip the scales of justice in favor of the weaker ones.

It is important for us to learn how power can work for us or against us. The first step in comprehending how power can work in our favor is to realize God is in control of the universe; hence we are under His authority. When we yield our capability to God, we will learn to respect His creation.

Man was not put on this earth to sit in judgement of anything or anyone. God calls for us to cover one another in His love. If we perceive ourselves to have abundant competence over someone else, we should strive to elevate that person.

It takes a real Christian to use their potential to be a champion of change. As we impart our knowledge, experiences, and skills to further the Great Commission in God's word; we begin to realize power is a tool which should be employed to help others seek God.

God has given us power and authority, so we may conquer the enemy. We must acquire knowledge in whom our enemy is, to be effective in our display of power. As we know, our enemy comes to "steal, kill, and destroy." (John 10:10) He is easily spotted, because he doesn't manifest himself in any new way.

Power is a gift from God; as a result, we should not disseminate our God-given potential without counting the cost. People will attempt to belittle us, so we can feel worthless or inferior. This is a trick of our enemy and he will employ any tactic necessary to keep us bound.

It is our duty to remember we have liberty, because we are God's chosen people. "We are fearfully and wonderfully made." (Psalms 139:14). We do not have to battle anyone, because God has already won for us.

Knowing when and how to use our power and authority comes by the wisdom of God. We must surrender to His plan and purpose in our life so that we can become effective agents of change. Never give up your God-given power.

By Lola Whidbee

INTRODUCTION

The secret things are referred to as the mysteries known by God. A secret is something hidden from others until it is known to the individual by way of revelation. A mystery is something unknown except through divine revelation. *Taking Back Your Power* is a book for everyone interested in understanding how to take back their power according to God's Word. It is a book that deals with the understanding of the blessings and favor of God. No one can be blessed with the favor of God unless they are in the right place and at the right time. Your experiences are determined by the ideas and thoughts in your mind, which is your heart, not the organ that is responsible for pumping the blood throughout your body. Your thought pattern flows to your mind's heart, which makes the revelation of God's power truthful within the inner man. All truth is power. When you release to God what is in your hand, He releases back to you what He controls with His hands. Giving demonstrates your level of faith. ***Hebrews 11:1 says, Now, faith is the substance of things hoped for, the evidence of things not seen.*** If you expect to receive from God His abundance, then you must learn to give abundantly to God. Your faith must be demonstrated by your giving. God cannot bless nothing. You must give God something to work with. The knowledge in this book will empower you to become the person who God created you to be. You will be encouraged to let go of your past and move into your future now. Your old way of thinking will be changed, and you will become the person you always were meant to be; but for whatever reasons you were afraid to accept the challenges and move forward into your destiny. I declare to you now you are getting ready to become unstuck and unshakeable.

Invest in yourself by feeding your mind the right thoughts that will empower you to become the best that you can be. To be able to take back your power, readers are encouraged to reflect upon each secret and journal their thoughts on how they intend to take back their power. This should be done with each secret and scripture references. All reflective thoughts should be written on the lines provided. Readers should reflect on their own personal life experiences as it relates to each secret and scripture references for each secret. Readers will learn some powerful truths as they continue to read through this book and take this journey with me. It is my sincere hope that you will become empowered, enlightened, and in your thinking, apply these secrets everyday of your life. Blessings!!!

Best wishes to all that will desire to read this book.

Dr. Terrence Parris

DON'T GIVE UP,
BECAUSE YOU CAN MAKE IT!

The Secret of Overcoming a Negative Mindset.

Today we are living in a world that is very discouraging. All around us, we can see how the values of the family have fallen away. Many of our families have a negative mindset. They just don't care about caring for anything. For some, they are pessimistic about everything in life. Nothing pleases them. For others, they are only negative when it comes to themselves and their own abilities. Either way, when you have a negative mindset, you cannot enjoy life the way you should; and as life should be for you to enjoy. You may even feel that it is very difficult and hard for you to maintain personal and work relationships.

It is a blessing to know that you can overcome a negative mindset and start enjoying the life that you were meant to have and experience. It is a matter of your choice and you recognizing the dangerous and harmful thought patterns that you bring to your own experience. You would need to determine what created those thought patterns and turn them off by replacing them with more effective, wholesome, and healthier thought patterns.

Reflective thoughts that will create change

Deuteronomy 31:6 Be strong and be of a good courage, fear not, nor be afraid of them: for the LORD thy God, he it is that doth go with thee; he will not fail thee, nor forsake thee.

_____

_____

_____

_____

_____

Where Do Your Negative Patterns Come From?

Many of our negative thought patterns were ingrained and instilled in us from very early in our life. As children growing up, sometimes we were raised in certain environments that did not employ an attitude of nurturing and encouragement. Also, at times we were very much unconscious of what was going on around us. We picked up worry over money from probably listening to our parents fight and fret about who were the boss and in charged. As time goes on, this worry about money became set in our psyche and it became a pattern of familiarity. So, when we think about money, we automatically begin to worry and develop pictures seeing everything that could possibly go wrong. This happens, because of our past experiences of our distant past growing up listening to and feeding on the negative thought patterns.

Reflective thoughts that will create change.

Proverbs 23:7 For as he thinketh in his heart, so is he: Eat and drink, saith he to thee; but his heart is not with thee.

_____

_____

_____

_____

_____

_____

_____

_____

_____

Don't You Ever Go There! But Go to the Place Called "There".

Do you know that it is much easier said than done? But don't allow yourself to become negative. As soon as negative thoughts begin to flood your mind, you need to stop them in their tracks and say to them, "there is no room in this house for you, so get away!" You see; unfortunately, much of our negative thought patterns are our inner dialogue which lies within our subconscious, so we are being negative without even knowing that we are negative. In other words, we set ourselves up for negative thinking at an early stage in life. In many cases, that negative dialogue is always present. Now, how can we not go there, but go to the place called **THERE**? Well, you need to begin with those situations in which you know you are being negative and stop the thoughts in their tracks.

Reflective thoughts that will create change.

Luke 6:45 A good man out of the good treasure of his heart bringeth forth that which is good; and an evil man out of the evil treasure of his heart bringeth forth that which is evil: for of the abundance of the heart his mouth speaketh.

_____

_____

_____

_____

_____

_____

_____

_____

You Must Take the Power Away from Negativity.

When you hear the negative thoughts turning around and around in your head, it is time to act. While many of our negative thoughts occur without us even knowing it, we are aware of some of these thoughts. As soon as you have a negative thought, stop the process. Take the power away from the negative thoughts and replace them with positive ones. For example, if you are thinking "I cannot do this!" Tell yourself, "I can do this if I try!" When you replace the negative thought with a positive thought, you will feel as though a 10,000 pound weight has been lifted off your shoulders. The key is to be consistent in replacing the negative thoughts with the positive ones. Do you see what I mean?

Reflective thoughts that will create change.

Philippians 4:13 I can do all things through Christ which strengtheneth me.

_____
_____
_____
_____
_____
_____
_____
_____
_____
_____

The Choice Is Always Yours to Make.

Whether you realize it or not, having a negative mind set is really a matter of choice. Making choices is very difficult for many people, but the reality is that many people don't want to hear this, but this is the gospel truth. Many people spend their whole life feeling imprisoned by negative thoughts and their emotions. The reality is that you need to make a choice about whether you want to be happy or whether you want to continue to be miserable with yourself. Decide right now what you want to do. Do you want to be happy with yourself or not? If you decide that you want to be happy, you can go forward knowing that your happiness is your goal and nothing in this world will stop you from being happy. You must be truthful about being happy to yourself. If not, you will not be dedicated to being happy by replacing the negative mindset with a positive mindset. It will become impossible to do so. Make the choice and stand by it. It will be beneficial in your near future.

Reflective thoughts that will create change.

Proverbs 17:22 A merry heart doeth good like a medicine: but a broken spirit drieth the bones.

Psalms 1:1-3 ¹Blessed is the man that walketh not in the counsel of the ungodly, nor standeth in the way of sinners, nor sitteth in the seat of the scornful. ²But his delight is in the Law of the LORD; and in his law doth he meditate day and night. ³And he shall be like a tree planted by the rivers of water, that bringeth forth his fruit in his season; his leaf also shall not wither; and whatsoever he doeth shall prosper.

_____

_____

_____

_____

Displace All Negative People Out of Your Life and Replace Them with Positive People.

If you are stuck in a negative mindset, chances are you are surrounded by like-minded people in your environment. Now! The old-adage that says, "misery loves company" is true. Therefore, when you find that you are in such a place of negativity, make a choice to change from that place. If you don't change positions, you will be attracted to all that negativity that surrounds you. When you surround yourself with negative people and situations, you will have a more difficult time changing your life. What you must do to get rid of negative people and situations? Delete all negative people and situations out of your life. Now, if there are situations that contribute to your negative mindset such as relationships or working environments, decide to work to change them or find a way out of the situation as soon as possible.

Reflective thoughts that will create change.

Proverbs 27:6 Faithful are the wounds of a friend; but the kisses of an enemy are deceitful.

Proverbs 13:20 He that walketh with wise men shall be wise: but a companion of fools shall be destroyed.

_____

_____

_____

_____

_____

_____

_____

_____

FAILURE IS NOT A CHOICE!

Learn to Welcome Criticism.

Many people fall into a negative mindset when they are criticized by someone. Whether you are criticized by someone you love or by someone that you don't like, you need to learn not to take it to heart. Instead, work to find the positive outcome in what you have been confronted with and told. Now! Instead of you looking at the situation from an overall character assassination, see the criticism and consider whether making a change will make you a better person, mate, coworker, or a better person in general. The message here is not to take criticism to heart; but instead you can consider it, think about it, reason with it, and then make the adjustments if necessary. After all is done, you move on knowing that you are a better person and not a bitter person.

Reflective thoughts that will create change.

Proverbs 15:32 He that refuseth instruction despiseth his own soul: but he that heareth reproof getteth understanding.

2 Timothy 3:16 All scripture is given by inspiration of God, and is profitable for doctrine, for reproof, for correction, for instruction in righteousness.

_____

_____

_____

_____

_____

_____

_____

Failure Is Not to be Feared, It is a Prerequisite to Your Success.

Many of the people that are successful today will tell you if you ask, that it was not exactly an easy road or journey getting where they are now. They will all have different stories to tell and do you know that these stories will not be all about big bonuses, success, and triumph. The many people that are embracing success now will tell you that they didn't get there overnight or in one day. It was a long journey through different kinds of obstacles and moving roadblocks. However, one thing all these people will likely tell you is that the hindrances and obstacles along the way were the motivating forces that pushed them and led them to their successes. Now! Failure should not always be viewed as negative. Failures are inevitable, and everyone gets to meet failure at some point in their life, but it does not mean that you have met a dead end. Failure is a learning tool. For example, when you are driving toward your destination and somehow get lost, because of a wrong turn and meet with a dead end, what you do is turn your vehicle around and continue driving in the right direction. Your failure or mistake was information given to you to change your direction, because you are going the wrong way and you cannot go any further, So, you will see that failure is not a bad thing, it can be positive. Sometimes wrong turns can lead you to a shortcut for the future. Those who are successful can surely tell of the role of setbacks and failures in their life.

Reflective thoughts that will create change.

Matthew 6:30 Wherefore, if God so clothe the grass of the field, which today is, and tomorrow is cast into the oven, shall he not much more clothe you, O ye of little faith?

_____

_____

_____

_____

Failure Will Wake You Up and Make You Strong.

Sometimes when everything is going our way, we tend to forget where we have come from, since we are having a very good time being at the top or on the way toward the top. Some people who almost tasted success, forgot their small beginnings and forgot the people who have helped them get there. In their carelessness and sometimes in their disobedience, they will meet impending falls and when this happens, they usually will collapse very hard. In this case, failure becomes a wakeup call that reminds you of your past or keeps you in focus with what use to be your goal. In the middle of your failures, you must separate yourself from the failures that will keep you grounded. There is an old saying my parents use to repeat all the time that goes like this "what don't kill you, will only make you stronger" and you know that is a true saying. When you survive after a great disaster, when you get stranded after a great calamity, such as hurricane Sandy, when you get to live after a momentous loss, when you have no place to lay your head, will you give up? No! This is, because you will come back even stronger than you were before.

Reflective thoughts that will create change.

Psalms 46:1-3 ¹God is our refuge and strength, a very present help in trouble. ²Therefore, will not we fear, though the earth be removed, and though the mountains be carried into the midst of the sea; ³Though the waters thereof roar and be troubled, though the mountains shake with the swelling thereof. Selah.

_____
_____
_____
_____
_____

Failure Makes Winning Feel Better and Taste Sweeter.

When you get the taste of success without much struggle, it does not feel like you deserve it. When you have received something that you vision for a long time finally get handed to you on a platter, the sensation and feelings are almost lost and becomes insignificant. You see failure makes success tastes sweeter and it will make you value the achievement even much more. It will make the challenges even more worthwhile that no one can take away from you. So, don't be afraid of failure, understand the lessons and learn from them. They are not meant to destroy and discourage you, but they are created to challenge you and to keep you going. Accept the bitter along with the sweet. Then you will know what is meant by the statement "failure makes winning taste better and sweeter."

Reflective thoughts that will create change.

Deuteronomy 31:6 Be strong and of a good courage, fear not, nor be afraid of them: for the LORD thy God, he it is that doth go with thee; he will not fail thee, nor forsake thee.

Psalms 32:7-8 ⁷Thou art my hiding place; thou shalt preserve me from trouble; thou shalt compass me about with songs of deliverance. Selah. ⁸I will instruct thee and teach thee in the way which thou shalt go: I will guide thee with mine eye.

_____

_____

_____

_____

_____

_____

_____

Failure Teaches Life Lessons.

When you fail in doing something that you want to do, it will be very painful; but it will also be one of life's learning experiences that you will learn. Because of that experience, you will find out which of the things to avoid so that you can do a better job the next time around. Failures are an important part of success, because it teaches values and disciplines that you will never learn otherwise. It will teach you all about hard work, humbleness, patience, humility; and of course, to be resilient. So, don't be afraid of mistakes, because they can be life's greatest teachers to move you on to your next level of life's journey. Be thankful for the failures in your life.

Reflective thoughts that will create change.

Galatians 5:22-23 [22]*But the fruit of the Spirit is love, joy, peace, longsuffering, gentleness, goodness, faith,* [23]*Meekness, temperance, against such there is no law.*

_____

_____

_____

_____

_____

_____

_____

_____

_____

Dealing With Your Personal Failures Effectively and Successfully.

Man is a human being and capable of making mistakes. Therefore, you are not alone in a perfect world. You will make mistakes. So, even if you think that you are a perfectionist, you cannot always avoid your errors or mistake from occurring. You see, what you can do is to take an assessment of what is going on in your life and take the necessary steps to correct that situation. You can be very careful not to make errors, but sometimes you are destined to approach a disaster that you did not prepare for. Again, mistakes are part of life experiences and if I can say, they are for the good of you. When you make a mistake, I want you to take three very long, deep breaths, and assess the area of your mistake. One of the most interesting and important thing about your situation is that you will find a way to overcome and recover from your mistakes at your advantage. So, don't worry about your failures. They are in your life to make you better not bitter.

Reflective thoughts that will create change.

Philippians 3:12-13 *¹²Not as though I had already attained, either were already perfect: but I follow after, if that I may apprehend that for which also I am apprehended of Christ Jesus. ¹³Brethren, I count not myself to have apprehended: but this one thing I do, forgetting those things which are behind, and reaching forth unto those things which are before.*

_____

_____

_____

_____

_____

You Must Overcome Your Negative Mindset.

A lot of people have a negative mindset. Negative mindsets come in different ways. With some people, it is their pessimistic attitude about everything in life. For others, they are only negative when it comes to themselves and their own abilities. You see either way, when you have a negative mindset, you cannot enjoy life the way you should, and you may even find that it is hard to keep and maintain personal and work relationships. It is a blessing to know that you can overcome any negative mindset and start enjoying the life that you were meant to have now. Let us be honest with ourselves. It is a matter of recognizing the harmful thought patterns, assessing the cause of them, and then turning them off, and substituting them with a more healthier patterns.

Reflective thoughts that will create change.

Proverbs 27:17 Iron sharpeneth iron; so a man sharpeneth the countenance of his friend.

You Can Overcome Your Failures by Developing the Right Mindset.

Quite a few people make a mockery at the power of the mind to influence circumstances, but many of them don't know that every achievement you make in life begins first in and foremost within the mind. Everything begins with a thought in the mind. So, if you constantly dwell on past failures and belittle yourself, it is like conditioning yourself to always be a failure. Now! How can you be successful when you cannot see yourself succeeding?

Your journey towards your success will not always be smooth. You will encounter many roadblocks along the way. These roadblocks will discourage you from wanting to move forward and at that point, you will have to make a choice whether to keep moving on or to give up and quit. In this journey, there will be many struggles that you will face along the pathway. If you only believe that the roadblocks that you face are only stepping stones to your future successes; don't become weak at the first obstacle that you face. Everything becomes possible when you believe it is possible. Your attitude will provide you with the strength that you need to move on and fight a good fight of faith.

Reflective thoughts that will create change.

Luke 10:27 And he answering said, Thou shall love the Lord thy God with all thy heart, and with all soul and with all thy strength, and with all thy mind; and thy neighbour as thyself.

_____

_____

_____

_____

MAKE YOUR WORK, WORK FOR YOU!

You Don't Have to be a Slave to Work.

The strategies of working smart and not hard have been around for ages. People think that if they can work long hours, then they will achieve much more success the easy way. It is said often that it is not about the quantity of work you put in, but rather the quality of the work which is done. You could be working 24 hours a day, without any rest, but achieve nothing significant to show for that length of time. At the same time, you could be working for just a few hours, but accomplish great things in that short span of time. You see, you do not have to be a slave to work to be able to achieve success. You just must know how to do the work smarter.

Reflective thoughts that will create change.

Luke 6:31 And as ye would that men should do to you, do ye also to them likewise.

Matthew 7:12 Therefore all things whatsoever ye would that men should do to you, do ye even so to them: for this is the law and the prophets.

_____
_____
_____
_____
_____
_____
_____
_____
_____

Your Work Does Not Have to Be Work.

Work is a drag for many people. It has become a dis-taste to others and detested by many. This happens, because work to many people is stressful and hard. The truth is work doesn't have to be work. It doesn't have to feel like it is a chore you dread. It is much better to find work in which you can feed your passion while you work. You see, if you love what you do, then you will be feeling good while you are doing it. So, make certain that you find the right work to do, something that you are passionate about, and everything else will move right in line with what you are doing. When your work is not work, then and only then, you can be passionate about what it is you are doing.

Reflective thoughts that will create change.

Colossians 3:23-24 [23]And whatsoever ye do, do it heartily, as to the Lord, and not unto men; [24]Knowing that of the Lord ye shall receive the reward of the inheritance: for ye serve the Lord Christ.

Just Go the Extra Miles, It Will Not Hurt.

Sometimes you will have to make decisions to go the extra mile by yourself. This is, because you will come to realize that not everyone can walk the path of the journey that was set for you. So, therefore you will have to go the extra mile by improving your mindset from the negativity of people, places, and things. Begin to see yourself as a master mind of the good you want for yourself. You can begin by telling yourself every morning "I am a very happy, healthy, and I have a positive life." If you begin to tell yourself this a couple of times a day, you will begin to believe just what you say. You see, just as you have taught and trained yourself to think of the worst of yourself and the world around you, you can think and train yourself to see your world from a better prospective, a more positive, more peaceful, gracious, and blessed world.

Reflective thoughts that will create change.

Ecclesiastes 9:10 Whatsoever thy hand findeth to do, do it with thy might; for there is no work, nor device, nor knowledge, nor wisdom, in the grave, whither thou goest.

_____

_____

_____

_____

_____

_____

_____

_____

_____

_____

When You Feel Overwhelmed, Consider Doing Some Meditation.

Whenever you start to feel the spirit of otherness around you, and negativity starts to linger and masks itself as something else, know what time it is. It is time to change those emotions and consider some meditation. I have found that meditation helps during those times of none stop emotions that are going nowhere and plays a major part in the development of your control of the negative emotions. In my practice, I have used various meditation methods, as well as self-help books to help learn the process of how to meditate effectively. You too can do the same.

Reflective thoughts that create change.

Psalms 119:15-16 [15]I will meditate in thy precepts, and have respect unto thy ways.

[16]I will delight myself in thy statues: I will not forget thy word.

Joshua 1:8 This book of the law shall not depart out of thy mouth; but thou shalt meditate therein day and night, that thou mayest observe to do according to all that is written therein: for then thou shalt make thy way prosperous, and then thou shalt have good success.

_____

_____

_____

_____

_____

_____

_____

Try Doing Positive Affirmations.

Many people have issues with whether positive affirmations work. My experience working with positive affirmations surely is a testimony. I can say boldly that it works wonders when you are trying to make better your negative mindset. What are positive affirmations? Positive affirmations are statements that help you change your perspective of the world and those around your world. For example, every morning and before you retire for the night, speak or think the affirmation. "I am a magnet of God's Love." The more love I share with others, the more I share God." Another example, "I am blessed, I am success, I am wealthy, I have more than enough." If you tell yourself positive things about yourself, after a while, you will start believing what you tell yourself. That is how positive affirmations work. It will work both negative and positive.

Reflective thoughts that will create change.

Philippians 4:19 But my God shall supply all your need according to his riches in glory by Christ Jesus.

Psalm 46:1 God is our refuge and strength, a very present help in trouble.

Isaiah 40:31 But they that wait upon the LORD shall renew their strength; they shall mount up with wings as eagles; they shall run, and not be weary; and they shall walk, and not faint.

_____

_____

_____

_____

_____

Fake It Until You Make It.

There is a strategy that has been around for decades that you probably heard about, that is the "fake it until you make it" philosophy. You need to put this "fake it until you make it" philosophy in place in your life until you make it. For example, if you put a smile on your face and you force yourself to look and feel happy, you will be happy. You see, many times just putting a smile on your face will help you begin to see the world, people, and places in a more positive outlook. Now, while you may not feel 100% positive about this faking it and making it strategy, faking it will take you a long way. When you fake it, you will begin to elicit positive vibrations and behaviors all around you, which will then draw more positive people to you and your situation and will only open avenues for helping you and strengthening your positive spirit.

Reflective thoughts that will create change.

Matthew 19:26 But Jesus beheld them, and said unto them, With men this is impossible; but with God all things are possible.

Job 42:2 I know that thou canst do everything, and that no thought can be withholden from thee.

_____

_____

_____

_____

_____

_____

_____

Making Positive Changes Is a Lifetime Habit.

If you are a person that is struggling with negative thoughts and mindsets, you can start to overcome them today by loving yourself and treating yourself with respect and dignity. When you accept being who you are and stop letting people tell you what you are, you are on the right path to start living a successful life. When you see yourself beginning to come out of your lost self, you need to keep up with the positive thoughts of whose you are and what it is that you are about, and where you are going. If you don't employ the positive affirmation about yourself every day, you will find yourself slowly falling back into the negative mindset. To remedy this, you should stay in close contact with positive people as much as you can and is allowed. By doing this, you will find that it is much easier to focus on the world in a much more positive and healthier manner. Remember to keep positive, stay healthy, laugh out loud, smile plentiful, learn from your mistakes, and always apologize for your mistakes and forgive yourself. In this game call life, there will be many misfortunes, but one thing you must remember, mistakes are tools of the trade, which helps you to learn and grow at the same time. Don't be afraid of your mistakes, welcome them!

Reflective thoughts that will create change.

Malachi 3:6 For I am the LORD, I change not; therefore, ye sons of Jacob are not consumed.

Numbers 23:19 God is not a man, that he should lie; neither the son of man, that he should repent: hath he said, and shall he not do it? or hath he spoken, and shall he not make it good?

Hebrews 13:8 Jesus Christ the same yesterday, and to day, and for ever.

_____

_____

_____

CONCLUSION

In conclusion, Taking Back Your Power (21) Secrets was not an easy task for me. During the process of writing this book, it served as a catharsis for me in which I was able to start the healing process, and transitioned from many negative mindsets that were totally devastating. Some of these setbacks were personal, social, emotional and financial. As the old negro spiritual song says, "Nobody Knows the Trouble I have seen." So, in life we all have had our share of setbacks, but this book is written as a self-help and motivational guide to help the reader to take back their power. By applying these secrets to your everyday life, it will assist you in becoming the person you always dreamed of being.

Understanding where the negative pattern comes from and taking control of them, you will be able to change your negative attitude and employ an attitude of encouragement. As soon as negative thoughts begin to flood your mind, you need to stop them in their tracks and say to them, "there is no room in this house for you so get away." Whether you realize it or not, having a negative mind set is really a matter of choice. When you must make a choice, make it and stand by it. It will be beneficial to you in your near future.

If you are stuck in a negative mind set, chances are you are surrounded by like-minded people in your environment. Remember the old-adage that says, "misery loves company" is a true testament. When you find yourself stuck in such a place of negativity, make a choice to change from that place. Remember to delete all negative people and places from your life.

You should not be afraid of failure. It is inevitable, and everyone gets the opportunity to meet with failure. Failure is a tool of learning. Your failure will not kill you, but it will make you stronger than you were before. Your failure will make your success sweeter, not bitter. Don't be afraid of your failures, face them while learning from them, and make the challenge more worthwhile.

Again, I must reiterate, don't be afraid of the mistakes you make, they are life's greatest teachers. Be thankful for the failures in your life. Your journey toward your success will not always be smooth, you will encounter hardship, and road blocks along the way. Everything becomes easier and possible when you believe it is possible. Your attitude will provide you with the strength you need to move on as you fight a good fight of faith. The truth about work is, when your work is not work, then and only then, you can be passionate about what you are doing.

Not everyone chooses to walk the straight and narrow path set before them, but often opt to find themselves following the crooked and wide path instead. Just as you have taught and trained yourself to think the worst of yourself and the world around you, you can think and train yourself to see your world from a better prospective, more positive, more peaceful, gracious and a blessed world.

Start employing positive affirmations over your life daily. Remember to keep positive, stay healthy, laugh out loud, smile as much as you can, forgive yourself of your mistake, and forgive others. Remember, you can only change what you confront. It is your life. Taking Back Your Power is your God given right.

www.ingramcontent.com/pod-product-compliance
Lightning Source LLC
LaVergne TN
LVHW021742060526
838200LV00052B/3428